T0198758

EXPLOSIVE IMPULSIVE ALLEY

AuthorHouse™
1663 Liberty Drive
Bloomington, IN 47403
www.authorhouse.com
Phone: 1 (800) 839-8640

Because of the dynamic nature of the Internet, any web addresses or links contained in
this book may have changed since publication and may no longer be valid. The views
expressed in this work are solely those of the author and do not necessarily reflect the views
of the publisher, and the publisher hereby disclaims any responsibility for them.

Any people depicted in stock imagery provided by Getty Images are models,
and such images are being used for illustrative purposes only.
Certain stock imagery © Getty Images.

This book is printed on acid-free paper.

ISBN: 978-1-7283-3725-8 (sc)
ISBN: 978-1-7283-3724-1 (e)

Library of Congress Control Number: 2019919862

Print information available on the last page.

Published by AuthorHouse 01/17/2020

authorHOUSE®

DEDICATION

We dedicate this book to the children and families across the world. You are loved; you are worthy; you are special; and you are beautiful. We encourage you to think positive thoughts, make positive affirmations, and love yourself and others.

We wish to ignite the endless possibilities of our children who have mental, learning, and behavior disabilities to help understand, explore, learn, cope, teach, grow, and support. *We love you!*

Explosive, Impulsive Alley

by
Quanteisha Ester and Jaela Denson

"Alley!"

Thump, thump, thump, thump. Alley could be heard jumping on the couch.

"Alley, stop jumping on the couch before you break your arm again!" yelled Alley's mom.

Boom! "Hahahahhahhaha!" Alley laughed as she fell to the floor.

Alley started to jump on the couch again.

"Mom, I love jumping on the couch. I love playing video games. I love telling funny jokes, and I *love* rollercoasters!" Alley said loudly. She was full of energy!

Boom! Bang! "Ouch! My bottom!" Alley said as she fell to the floor again. Alley's mom rushed to find Alley flat on her bottom, laughing.

"You're going to hurt yourself, sweetheart. Please settle down! You have a lot of energy, and your teacher called today. That's the second time this week," said Mom.

"I know; I'm sorry. Mom, am I bad?" asked Alley.

"No, Alley, of course not. You're just impulsive." Answered Mom

"What's impulsive?" asked Alley.

"Impulsive is when you do things or react without thinking it out."

"You know, like when you ran and jumped off the chair and broke your arm," said Mom as she sighed.

"Hahahaha!" Alley laughed.

"Or like when I thought I was a superhero in the grocery store, and I knocked over all the spaghetti sauce in the aisle!" hahahhhahhah laughed Alley

"Oh, like when I was at the doctor's office and I was running and I knocked over the fish tank, and all the fish were all over the floor, flapping. Hahahhhahahahahahahhahaha!" Alley burst into laughter.

"Okay, baby. Yes, those are goo—Alley, please don't stand on the chair.

Alley, please get down and sit still.

Alley, please don't drop the chair.

Alley, please settle down. *Alley!*" huffed Mom.

"But I don't want to!" said Alley. "I don't like to sit in one spot like you have to at school. It makes me feel like I'm going to explode!" Alley was very hyper.

"Alley, sometimes you have to sit still, especially in school while the teacher is teaching." Said mom!

"That's boring," said Alley, and then she laughed.

"What does explode mean to you, Alley?" asked Mom.

"Like when I don't like something, I get frustrated, upset, or sad."

"What other things make you feel like you want to explode?" asked Mom.

"Or like when I got in trouble at school for blurting out, 'Sara's feet smell!' and I had to leave the class—I got upset, and I felt like I wanted to explode. That's not fair! I always get in trouble." Alley said sadly

"Or like when the babysitter calls you while you're at work to tell you that I'm not doing so well—it makes me upset."

"I don't do anything wrong, Mom." Alley says sadly

"Ooohh or when you take my video game from me when I get in trouble—I feel hurt, like I want to explode," said Alley.

"I know, Alley, but there are rules to follow," said Mom.

"I know, Alley; there are rules to follow." Alley responded in a mocking tone, and then she laughed.

"Alley, stop mocking me," said Mom.

"Alley, stop mocking me," responded Alley in a mocking tone.

"Alley, stop it, please," said Mom.

"Alley, stop it please," said Alley as she laughed.

"Alley, stop it now!" said frustrated Mom

"We have to start getting ready for dinner, homework, bath, and bed. But first, you have to clean your room," Mom said.

Alley looked off in space.

"Alley, are you listening to me?" asked Mom.

"Mom, can I have a bike? Can I go to dance? Can I have ice cream if I'm good in school?" screamed Alley.

"Honey, that's not what we are talking about. Alley, please have a seat. Alley, you're going to break something. Alley, don't run in the house. Alley, stop, please! Alley, *no! Alley!*" yelled Mom. "Alley, go clean your *room now!*" said her frustrated mom.

Alley went into her room and started playing with her toys.

"Alley, I hope you're cleaning up your room!" yelled Mom.

"Okay, okay, Mom," said Alley.

Alley's mom went into Alley's room and found Alley's toys all over the floor, and Alley was jumping on the bed.

"Alley, honey, your room isn't clean, and you still have to do homework, eat dinner, take a bath, and go to bed."

"Oh, I'm sorry, Mommy!" exclaimed Alley.

"Alley, get down. Alley, don't throw the toy. Alley, stop jumping. Alley, please calm down. Alley, come eat your dinner. Alley, please put the toys away and go wash your hands for dinner!" said Mom angrily.

As Alley got ready for her nightly routine, she became more and more difficult.

At dinner, Mom said, "Alley, sit and eat your food. Alley, please sit still. Alley, don't spill your food. Alley, don't lean back in your chair. Alley, don't eat with your hands. Alley, go wash your hands, and get ready for your homework, please."

"Ew, Mom. You have a booger in your nose." Alley laughed.

"Alley, wash your hands now," Mom said in a serious tone.

During homework time, Alley said nervously, "I lost my glasses. Oh, my."

"Alley, your glasses are right on the table," Mom said.

"Oh, right!" exclaimed Alley. "Mom, do bugs have funerals when they die?"

"Alley, focus on your homework, p l e a s e ," Mom said.

"M o m, my arm itches," said Alley.

"Alley, finish your homework, and stop squirming, please," said Mom.

"Mom, can I go play laser tag?" asked Alley. "Mom, I'm sleepy. I don't want to do this. Mom, can I have ice cream? Mom, can I be a monster for Halloween? *Mom!*"

"Alley, please focus on your work so we can bathe and get ready for bed."

"But ..."

"Alley, focus, honey," said Mom.

At bath time, Mom said, "Alley, please stop splashing water on the floor. Alley, don't throw you dolls in the toilet. Alley, you must stay in the bath. Alley, please stop. *Alley!*"

Bang! Boom! Mom slipped on water on the bathroom floor, and Alley let out a big laugh. "Alley, that's not funny. Get out, dry off, and go to your bed *now!*"

It was bedtime. "Alley, I hope you are going to have a better day at school tomorrow. Today was an explosive, impulsive day," Mom said.

"I know, Mom. I'm sorry. I want to do better, but sometimes my brain moves so fast, and it makes my body move fast so I can't sit still. Then I get in trouble," said Alley.

"How does that make you feel?" asked Mom.

"It really hurts my feelings when people at school treat me different because I get in trouble a lot," Alley said sadly. "It's really hard for me. I just want to be a normal kid, Mom," Alley pleaded.

"Hey, Alley, don't think that way. We think positive, and I want you to know you are a limited edition!"

"What's that?" asked Alley.

"You know, someone who's rare to find but everyone wants to have. You're the most amazing, smart, funny, playful, loving kid I know. And I love you in every way," said Mom.

"Mom, I know we have the special things at school for me, but is there anything else we can try? I don't want to be explosive and impulsive anymore," said Alley.

"Yes, we can try some other things to help you, Alley. Why don't you get some rest, and I'll think of something," said Mom.

After a long day, Mom thought all night about how to help Alley improve her behavior and learning. Mom searched long and hard for a solution for Alley.

"I have it!" said Mom. It was like a lightbulb went off in her head. "I'll create a program!" Mom said proudly.

Morning Routine

- Brush Teeth
- Take Vitamin
- Take Bath
- Comb Hair
- Break Fast
- Get Dress
- Go to School

Alleys Activities

Music Therapy
Art Therapy
Meditation, Yoga
Educational Programs
Learning Activities

Night Routine

- Dinner
- Take Vitamin
- Take Bath
- Comb Hair
- Get pajamas
- Go to Bed

Mom created a program that helped all Alley's challenges. The program included meditation (mindfulness) to help Alley with focus, calm, and clarity. Music and art therapy helped reduce hyperactivity and strengthen social skills. Aromatherapy (essential oils) helped Alley sleep, pay attention, and relax. Yoga helped Alley's self-control, concentration, confidence, and calm. Educational and learning activities helped Alley's behavior and taught her to focus and learn better.

The next day, Alley's mom called her school and got everyone involved in her program.

Soon after, Alley's friends, teachers, sitter, pediatrician, and mom all saw a huge change in her behavior and learning.

Alley loved her new program. She now has a lot of friends. Her grades are good, and she no longer has trouble or is called explosive and impulsive. She now enjoys the name Amazing-Acting Alley.

MY REASON

Infinite Stars Incorporation

As parents, we dream of the best for our children. Intrinsically, we want to protect them from the world. As parents, we are novices, blindfolded on voyages that have undoubtedly proven to be tumultuous with astounding accuracy. How do we keep going? We're all given a reason —something that keeps us going when we want to give up!

My reason's name is Jaela Marie Denson. Jaela has to be the most affable, loving, intelligent, compassionate kid I've ever had the pleasure of coming across. She loves to play video games, is very social, and tells a lot of jokes. One day, at the young age of five, our lives changed. Jaela was diagnosed with ADHD and a learning disability. Jaela showed signs of impulsiveness, inability to focus, forgetfulness, daydreaming, distractedness, interrupting others, squirming, fidgeting, sensitivity to sound, aggressive behavior, difficulty following direction, inability to focus in structured environments, and a lack of organizational skills as early as three. She was like a Tasmanian devil in large groups. It wasn't until she got to school that it became conspicuous not only to myself, but also to her teachers and peers.

I inevitably went to seek help from her pediatrician. The pediatrician recommended that I put her on medication to help with focus in school and that she be seen by a therapist. To hear the news of medication startled me. Not only was I *not* educated on the different types of medication and side effects, but I also had no clue how to give a five-year-old a capsule. The therapy may have proved effective, but as a single parent, I was missing a lot of work, and she was missing a lot of school. Things didn't get any better after the diagnoses.

For years, we tried everything with little to no results. The medication we tried made Jaela like a zombie. She lost weight, slept too much or not at all, complained about headaches, had stomachaches, experienced muscle aches, vomited, had hives, and was dehydrated, and it offset her pH balance terribly.

ADHD falsely misrepresents a person. Jaela soon became the loose cannon who tantalized her peers and exhausted her teachers, doctors, and sitters. I was out of options. We experienced changing schools; suspension; a plethora of phone calls from schools, parents, and neighbors; and complaint after complaint. We avoided activities with friends. She was bullied, taunted, put into special restrictive programs in school, and sent to hundreds of school meetings. Special accommodations were made for everything, and we were unable to keep a sitter.

Tears filled my eyes, and stress wasn't the word. Seeing a therapist for myself and hiding at home were all I knew. One day, as I did many times before, I was searching the web for a program to fit my needs as a parent and to help alleviate the stress and medication for Jaela. I was looking for an organization that understood that there is an underlying issue and whose goal is to get to the root of the problem and execute. My search was unsuccessful. Desolated, lost, and in despair, I manifested a great blessing.

"Create a program," I said to myself. Ideas began pouring in! I bought tons of books; I read even more on different disabilities and the impact they have on families. I became an advocate; the energy was invigorating. I studied night and day. One day, I decided to go back to school. I then became a holistic health doctor for alternative medicine. That led me to create Infinite Stars Inc., an organization with hope and healing. The organization seeks to help ignite endless possibilities for children who have unique mental, behavior, and learning needs and to help others understand, learn, cope, teach, grow, support, and explore with a patient and understanding educational environment. Today, Jaela is a ten-year-old. She is imaginative, fun, energetic, charismatic, daring, inquisitive, courageous, and full of love. She has goals and aspirations so astronomical that they will need their own zip code. My reason taught me that if you reach for the stars and come up short, then create your own constellation!

Thank you so much for reading.

ABOUT INFINITE STARS

Infinite Stars Incorporation is a nonprofit organization founded in 2015.
We provide healing and growth for children who have mental, behavior, and learning disabilities with a holistic approach.

Our goal at Infinite Stars Inc. is to systematically transform the minds, beliefs, and environments of children and families who have mental, behavior, and learning disabilities. We offer support, comprehensive educational programs, workshops, holistic and medicine alternatives, therapy, reconstructing family dynamics, youth groups, and much more.

All our programs accentuate the individual diagnoses and are instrumental in conducting great results.

Infinite Stars Inc.'s key components strengthen the underlying core weakness of each subjective diagnosis and seek to obliterate medication or leave it only as an option, help eradicate the stress off the family, and place children in an exciting, fun, loving, educational environment.

We insist on the transition into public school and everyday life.

Our children at Infinite Stars will strive with holistic alternatives and educational programs that are individual to each child. These programs are based on their unique developmental profiles and patterns and are designed to aid them in reaching higher levels of learning and behavior. We provide a patient and positive environment that understands and leaves medication only as an option.

We ignite endless possibilities for our children and families with guaranteed results.

Find us at:

www.Infinitestars.org

Instagram @InfiniteStarsInc

Facebook @Infinitestarsincorporation

Youtube @Infinitestarsinc

DISABILITY FACTS

6.4 Million children in the U.S are diagnosed with ADD/HD 4-17 years of age.

42% increase in ADD/HD diagnosis over the past 8 years.

6.1% of American children are being treated for ADD/HD with medication.

ADD/HD can continue into adulthood especially if not treated

Boys have a higher percentage than girls, girls tend to go undiagnosed for ADD/HD

Children with ADD/HD have concerns with social interactions with peers. 3x as many peer problems. 10x more issues related friendships will mess up their self esteem

Some signs of ADD/HD are: Trouble sleeping, impulsive behavior, daydreaming, trouble paying attention or focusing on a task, very easily distracted, forgetful, very talkative, interactive, squirm/fidget, don't listen or follow directions, speak and act without thinking.

42.5 Billion dollars is spent on ADD/HD per year averaging about $14,576 per person a year.

ADD/HD is hereditary, 40% of children with it has at least one parent with it.

ADD/HD does happen due to bad parenting, watching television, or picking it up from others.

Many children who do not get over it by the age od12 carry ADHD into adulthood.

A learning Difficulty is not a disorder

Learning Difficulties affect people of all ages

A growing percentage of children with learning disabilities drop out of high school

3 million children ages 6-21 have some form of learning disability.

There are 7 different types of learning styles: Visual (spatial), Aural (auditory-Musical), Verbal (linguistic), Physical (kinesthetic), logical (mathematical), Social (interpersonal), Solitary (intrapersonal)

There are over 10 different learning difficulties: Auditory Processing, Dyscalculia, Dysgraphia, Dyslexia, Language Processing, Non-verbal learning difficulty, Visual Perceptual/Visual Motor Deficit, ADHD, Dyspraxia, Executive Functioning, and Memory

Only 10% of students with a Learning Difficulty are enrolled in a four-year college within 2 years of leaving school.

Among working-age adults with LD only 50% are employed

Learning Difficulties vary from person to person. One person may not have the same kind of learning problems as another person with LD.

Persons with LD were 2 to 3 times more likely to report fair to poor physical, general, and mental health.

6% of students in regular schools are receiving special education programs or services because of learning difficulties.

9.4% of children aged 2-17 years (approximately 6.1 million) have received an AHDH diagnosis

7.4% of children aged 3-17 years (approximately 4.5 million) have a diagnosed behavior problem

7.1% of children ages 3-17 years (approximately 4.4 million) have diagnosed anxiety.

3.2% of children aged 3-17 years (approximately 1.9 million) have diagnosed depression.

Having another disorder present in very common with children with disabilities it's called a comorbidity; 90% of children with ADHD (Attention Deficit Hyperactivity Disorder) have ODD (Oppositional Defiant Disorder). 3 in 4 (73%) children with depression also have anxiety and 1 in 2 (47.2%) also have behavior problems.

For children aged 3-17 years with anxiety, more than 1 in 3 (37.9%) also have behavior problems and about 1 in 3 (32.3%) also have depression.

For children aged 3-17 years with behavior problems, more than 1 in 3 (36.6%) also has anxiety and about 1 in 5 (20.3%) also have depression.

There is almost a 14% increase in anxiety and depression in children ages 6-17 in 2019

Anxiety diagnosis has increased from 6.4% in 2012 to 9.6% in 2019

Depression diagnosis has increased from 4.9% in 2012 to 5.6% in 2019

70% of children and adolescents who experience mental health problems have not had appropriate interventions at a sufficiently early age.

Nearly 8 in 10 children (78.1%) ages 3-17 years with depression received treatment.

6 in 10 children (59.3%) age 3-17 years with anxiety received treatment

More than 5 in 10 children (53.5%) age 3-17 years with behavior disorder received treatment.

1-6 (17.4%) children in the U.S aged 2-8 years has a mental, behavior, or a developmental disorder.

Diagnosis of depression and anxiety are more common with increased age

Behavior problems are more common among aged 6-11 years than children younger or older

Among children aged 2-8 years, boys were more likely than girls to have a mental, behavior or developmental disorder.

Among children living below 100% of the federal poverty level, more than 1 in 5 (22%) had a mental, behavior or developmental disorder.

Age and Poverty level affected the likelihood of children receiving treatment for anxiety, depression, or behavior problems.

ABOUT THE AUTHORS

Quanteisha Marie Ester is a mom who wanted to give children a voice, a platform, and an outlet. She thought writing was the best way to convey these things. Quanteisha and her ten-year-old daughter Jaela have written many books together as a family. They wanted to raise awareness of mental disabilities and shed light on the effects they have on families and the community.

Quanteisha Marie Ester was born and raised in little Rock, Arkansas. In 2002, at age fourteen, Quanteisha and her family moved to Kansas City, Kansas. She graduated from high school in 2006 with a basketball scholarship; she then went to college, where she studied criminal justice. After college, Quanteisha put her abilities into going to school to be a train conductor. In 2008, she began a career at BNSF Railway, where she currently works.

In 2009, Quanteisha gave birth to an amazing little girl by the name of Jaela. Early on, she knew Jaela was a beautiful, special gift. Jaela was diagnosed with attention deficit hyperactivity disorder (ADHD) in 2015 but showed signs as early as three years old.

After exhausting all her options, Quanteisha founded Infinite Stars Incorporation, a nonprofit organization for children who have mental, behavioral, and learning disabilities. The organization raises awareness for children and families who share similar unique diagnoses.

Quanteisha furthered her knowledge and educated herself on mental and behavioral health in ways that benefit her, Jaela, her community, and families all over the world. She is a holistic health practitioner certified in meditation, crystal therapy, detoxification, and aromatherapy. She is an herbalist, spiritual guided counselor, life coach and speaker. She is certified in reiki I and II and much more.

Quanteisha Ester is a vegan woman who possess a heart of gold. She is very ambitious and has innate abilities, talents, and many spiritual gifts. She believes in systematically transforming the minds, beliefs, and environments of children and families who have mental, behavioral, and learning disabilities. She is instrumental in introducing and igniting endless possibilities by implementing holistic alternatives, effective programs, and educated and resourceful environments for the success and growth of our children.

With love, positivity, encouragement, motivation, confidence, and compassion she guarantees the individual growth and success of our children in a life-changing environment with Infinite Stars Inc., where we ignite endless possibilities.

Jaela Marie Denson was born in Overland Park, Kansas on August 18, 2009. She is in the fourth grade and enjoys spelling, reading, writing, and playing with friends. She enjoys playing video games, music, roller coasters, theme parks, fun, adventure, and doing fun activities with her mother. Jaela has a heart of gold; she is very inquisitive and wants nothing but to shower everyone with love. Jaela dreams of one day becoming an entrepreneur, as she wants to make a difference in her community and the world!

Jaela wanted to share her story of having ADHD with the world by writing a book on her everyday struggles and difficulties and the influence it had on her life, her mom, and her community. She hopes to help children and families all across the world know that there is an answer and that they are loved, valued, worthy, and wanted. You are her friend, and she accepts you for you.

Printed in the United States
By Bookmasters